Just Let Me Color

Rebecca Harrison

Samantha Metting

iUniverse®

JUST LET ME COLOR

iUniverse books may be ordered through booksellers or by contacting:

iUniverse
1663 Liberty Drive
Bloomington, IN 47403
www.iuniverse.com
1-800-Authors (1-800-288-4677)

Artist's Note:
Depending on the medium that you have chosen to color with, I would suggest that you place a page of card stock or your choice paper so that you can stop any potential bleed through of certain types of ink. Happy coloring!

ISBN: 978-1-4917-8346-7 (sc)
ISBN: 978-1-4917-8347-4 (e)

Library of Congress Control Number: 2015919436

Print information available on the last page.

iUniverse rev. date: 11/23/2015

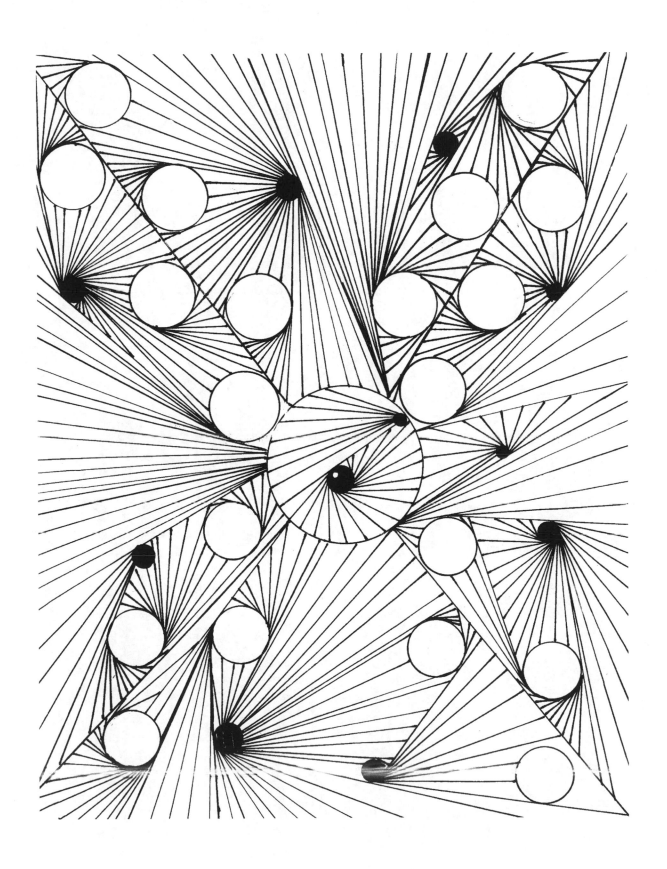

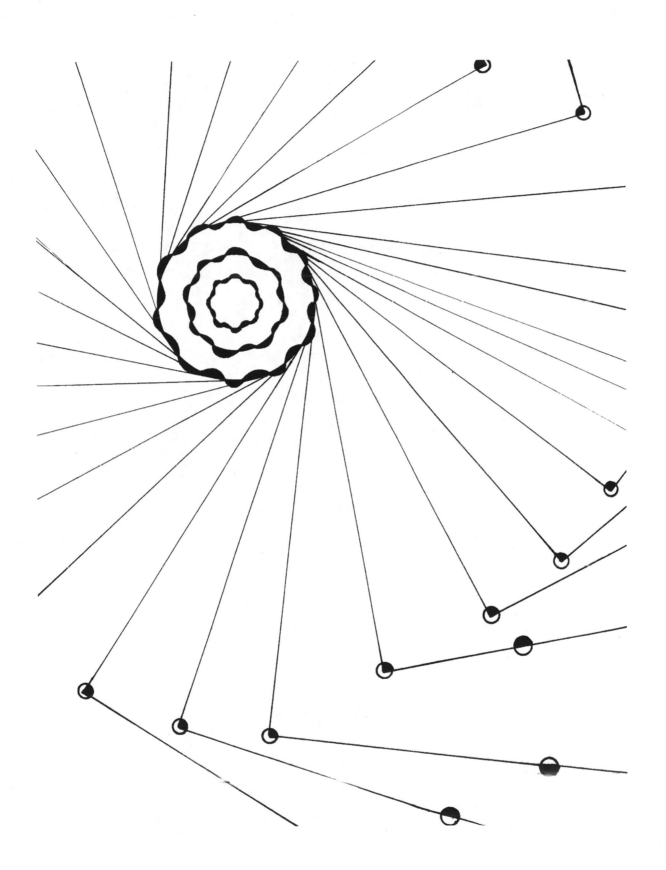

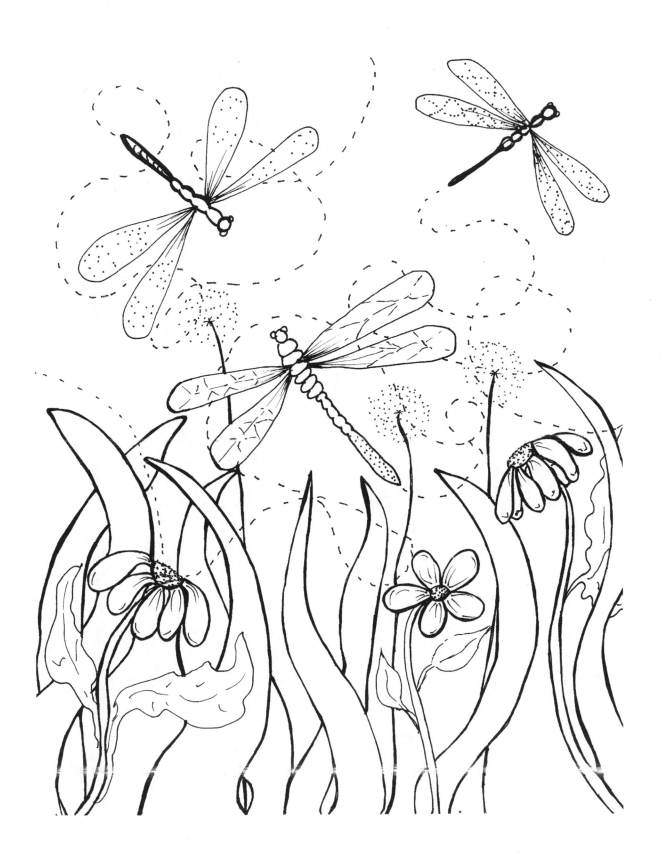

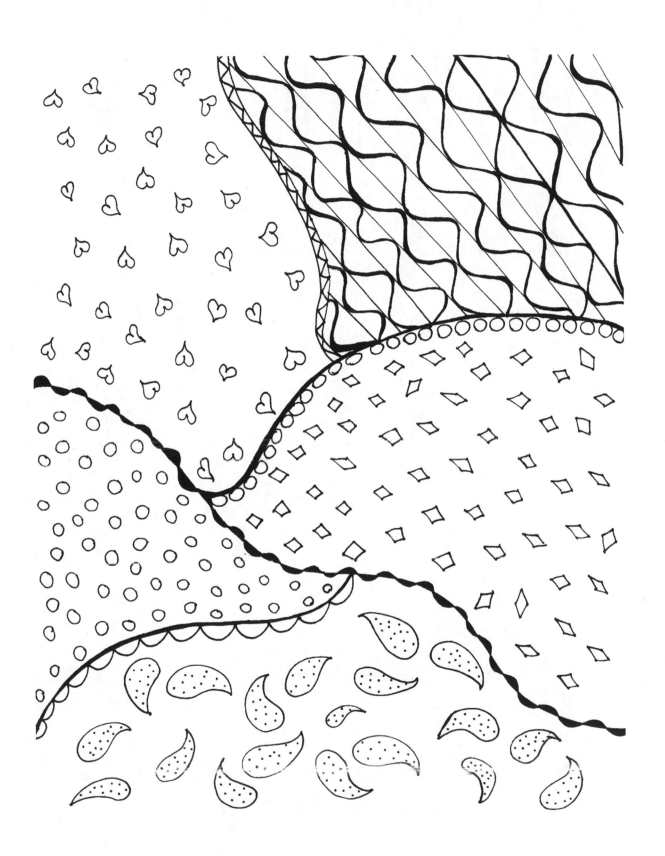

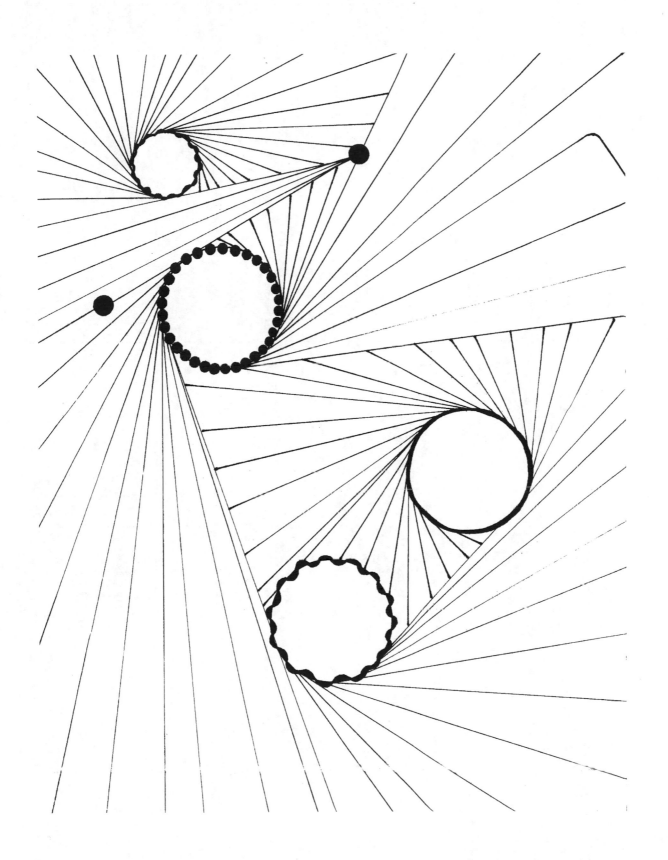

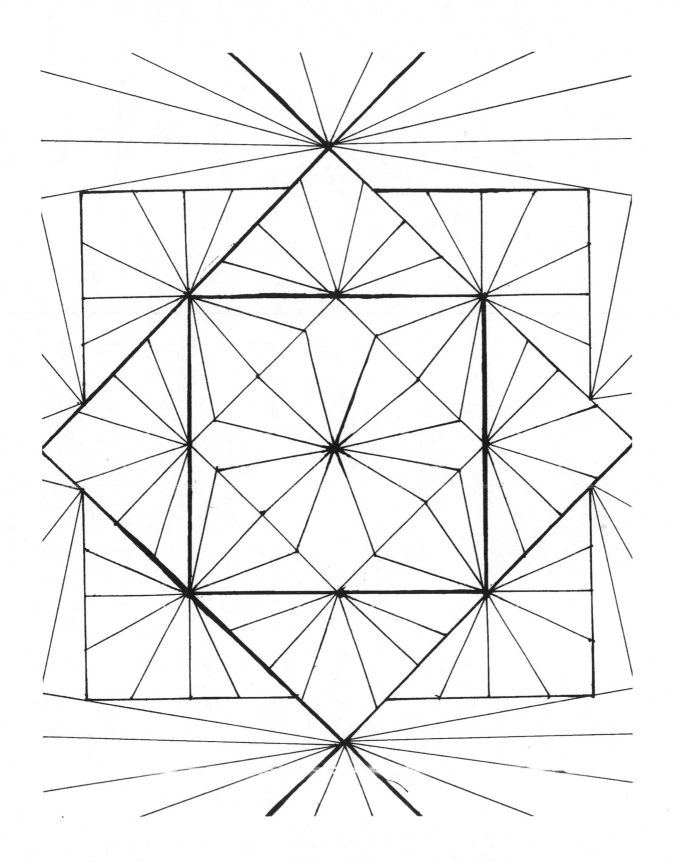

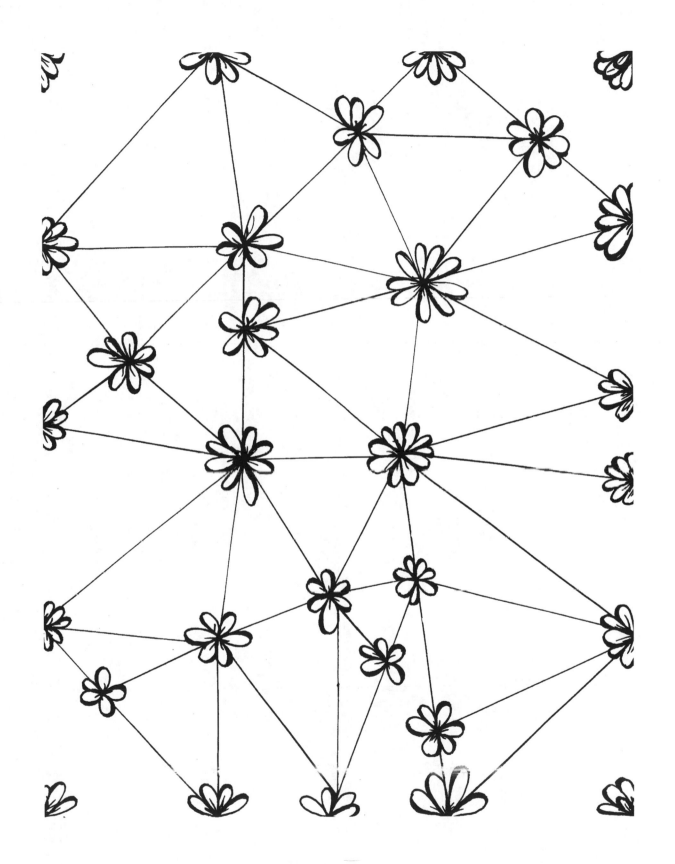

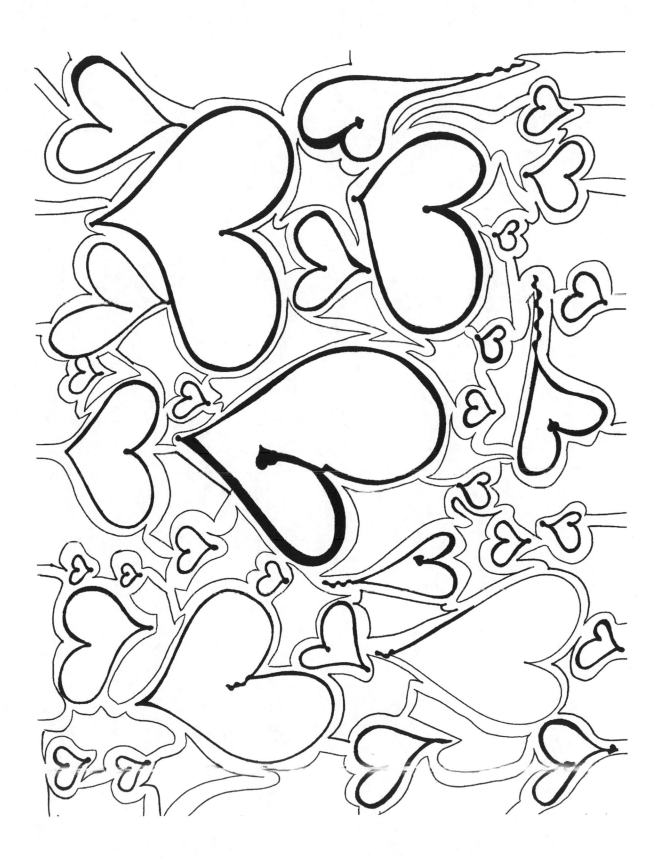

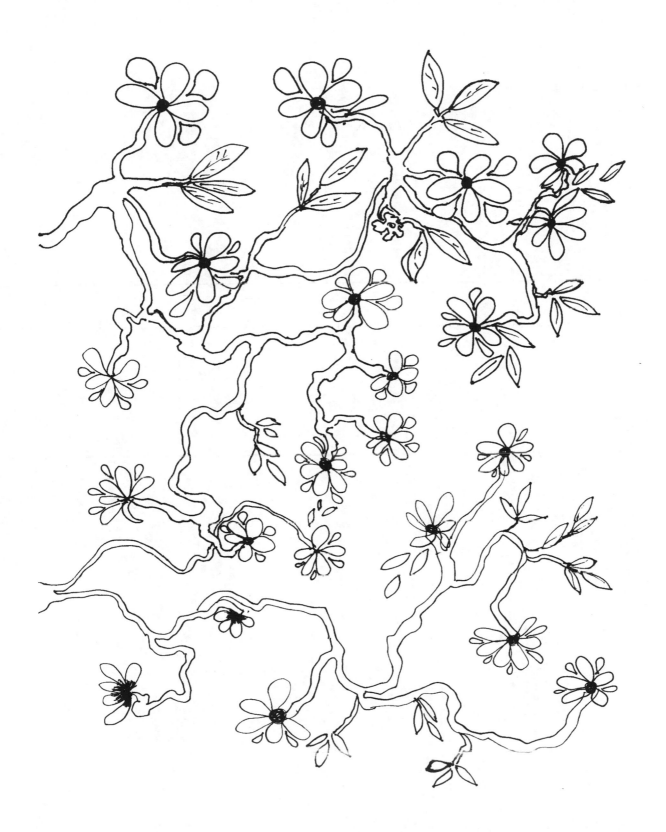

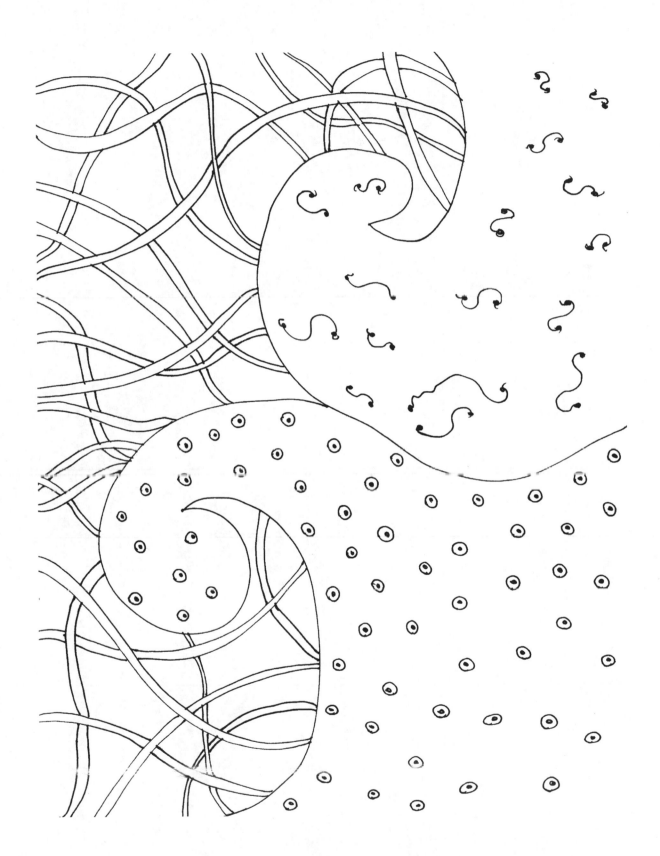

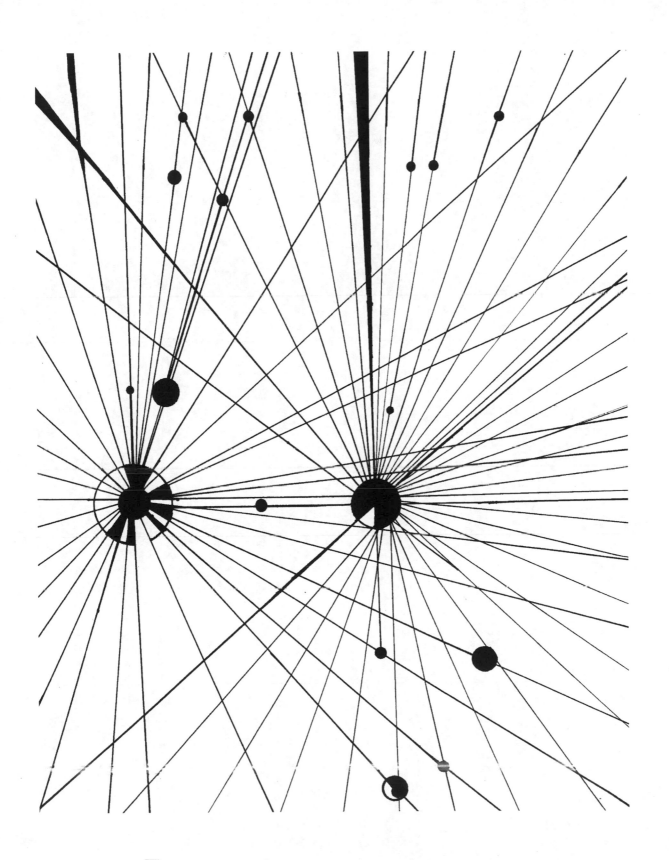

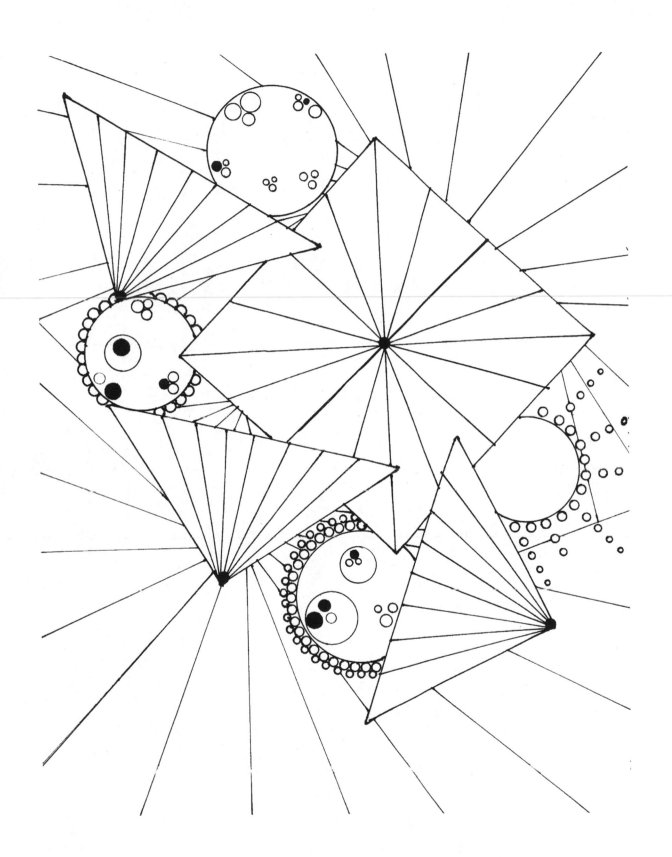

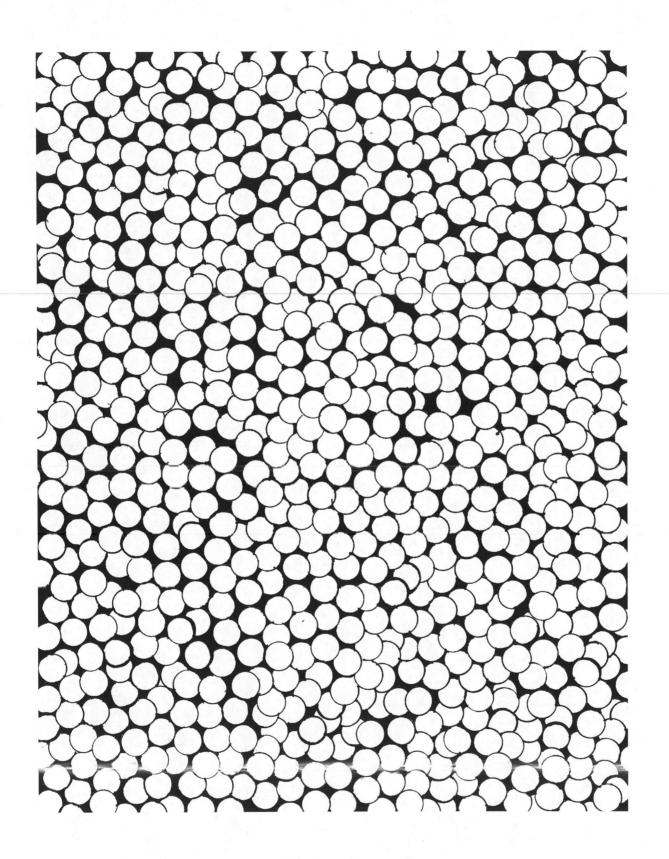

Printed in the United States
By Bookmasters